Manifest Wealth & Abundance

Jen Ward

Jen Ward

CONTENTS

Jen Ward

MANIFEST WEALTH & ABUNDANCE

Why I Want To Be "Well-Thee"

I make no apologies for wanting to be rich. Light workers, healers and do-gooders feel ashamed for wanting this for themselves. It is as if they don't deserve it or they feel like a sellout for wanting to be wealthy.

I want to be rich, but not by taking from others. I want to get rich by giving so much of myself and doing what I love that being rich is a natural consequence that follows. I want to be rich as a natural reflection of my abundant state. I want to be very rich as a way to show to others what being rich with no shame and no arrogance looks like. Being "well-thee" is a declaration of a kind and thoughtful life with respect for all others.

I want to be rich to teach others what being rich looks like. That it isn't about stepping on the throats of others or being gaudy as a show of wealth. It isn't about fast cars or expensive, showy shoes. It's about being so comfortable in your skin and loving life so much that abundance is a byproduct of your loving state of gratitude and acceptance. It is a means to empower the things in this world that matter like nature, freedom, education and sustainability.

Yes, being rich is very important to me. Others need to see that being rich is nothing to be ashamed of. Abundance isn't evil and those who have it do not need to come by it through lying, cheating, taking or stealing. Abundance is a mainframe of a grateful, fulfilled life. More good and empowerment can come through being rich than claiming false humility and poverty.

If you want to be rich, you don't get there by saying how poor you are or cursing others. You do so by being grateful that abundance exists, and you are aware enough to realize that if one person has it, it is possible for everyone. You learn to use your special gifts and qualities in such a unique way that wealth is inevitable. You also are benevolent and caring to all who want to be empowered too. You never allow anyone to be a victim by claiming to be too sick or poor to be wealthy. You reward those who understand they are empowered but are still figuring out their way.

I want to pour as much wealth back into the world as possible, literally. I want to grow trees and buy land and create forests. I want to teach others how to listen to trees, invest in products that sustain the planet, grow a voice that is heard and respected, see all those I love become abundant beyond their wildest dreams, and empower everyone to have a voice, uncover their greatness, share their gifts, unabashedly share their truth and claim their own worth. There is too much of the opposite going on and it ends now!

The main reason I want to be rich is to give permission to all those who feel they need it to accept their own wealth. Also to provide a blueprint of how to become "well-thee" while empowering others, blessing the world and creating "well-thee" people wherever we go and with whatever we lovingly do.

Release the Aversion to Money

Most people think that they would welcome a windfall if it landed in their lap but what they don't realize is that they set up their own dynamic with money. If people are not attracting something in their life, they are the ones repelling it.

In private sessions such things as believing money is the root of all evil, or that only selfish, powerful people have money, have kept many from attracting it to themselves. There was one client who, in a past life, was so disgusted by the behavior of the rich that they vowed never to have money because they didn't want to abuse power. These latent dynamics prevent monetary abundance from flowing in this life.

In sessions we comb out the dynamics with money on all levels. Many times, the client will get evidence that the session was effective almost immediately. They will suddenly get a tax refund, a client will pay them unexpectedly, or they will get an opportunity to earn more. The important thing to realize is to NOT set your standards on what to expect by what society as a group is agreeing to accept. You in your empowerment can choose to be the exception to every rule of conformity that limits your personal wealth.

In many of my sessions, I deal with abundance. It is surprising how many people have an aversion to their own wealth. It is either out of unworthiness, conceptualizing monetary gain as negative, or just by feeling generally overwhelmed. It is really wonderful to be able to help people undo the damage they inflict upon themselves and the aversion to their own blessings.

I have worked on releasing the issues of abundance with a long time client, yet they still were showing up in his life. We tuned in to the issue in a recent session. Core beliefs preventing him from having monetary wealth revealed themselves.

The first issue was his preference for bartering. He had a strong opinion about money and definitely felt bartering was better. Even though we released all his aversion to money in past sessions, we now had to release his preference for bartering. He had to stop micromanaging the Universe and how abundance came to him.

The SFT tap I led him through was, "I release needing my abundance to be converted into the barter system, in all moments." It actually felt like the Universe was sitting on a whole stockpile of his abundance and was working diligently on converting it into barter.

The second issue was a dislike of banks and bankers. This was the true bottleneck to him being rich. In our work, we got to the point where he was willing to accept monetary gain, but now the deeper issue was that he would have to deal with the banks and bankers. In many lifetimes, he saw them as the enemy. We released all his aversions to bankers and helped him be receptive to having a relationship with them. The bottleneck was opened.

Abundance, just like love, is a birthright. If everyone else agrees on some level to push love and abundance away, you do not have to agree. This is the personal component of being your own person.

Here is a series of taps to help attract the money that you may have set up to repel.

How to say the taps: Say the following statements three times while tapping on the top of your head at the crown chakra. Then say them a fourth time while tapping on your chest at the heart chakra. Say each word deliberately. They are not just words but a vibration that you are initiating to shift energy. Pause after each word. Say it in a commanding but even tone, not as a question. Forgo saying it in a singsong tone or with bravado. Say them all.

"I release hating money; in all moments."

"I release the belief that money is evil; in all moments."

"I release defining money as an abuse of power; in all moments."

"I remove all curses between myself and money; in all moments."

(A curse is any negative statement charged with emotion.)

"I release feeling shame around having money; in all moments."

"I release repelling money; in all moments."

"I release the belief that I am unworthy of money; in all moments."

"I release the fear of having money; in all moments."

"I release the belief that I am unworthy to have money; in all moments."

"I make space in this world to have an abundance of money; in all moments."

"I remove all blockages to having money; in all moments."

"I stretch my capacity to have an abundance of money; in all moments."

"I am centered and empowered in having an abundance of money; in all moments."

If you can shift this in your life, you can shift many other things as well.

Releasing Beliefs Around Poverty

It is surprising how many good, spiritual people are not living in abundance. It seems that those who lead a good life, and are kind and loving to others, would naturally attract wealth. To me, spirituality is joy, love, abundance, freedom and wholeness.

People are empowered to manifest more than they realize. If they are not having a life filled with joy, love, abundance, freedom and wholeness, it may be their misconception of what God expects of them. In past times, a life of self-denial may have been expected. Maybe that old belief system is still ingrained somewhere in the psyche. If so, here is assistance in releasing it.

(Say each statement three times while tapping on your head and say it a fourth time while tapping on your chest.)

"I release the belief that God wants me to be poor; in all moments."

"I release the belief that God wants me to suffer; in all moments."

"I release the belief that God wants me to martyr myself; in all moments."

"I release the belief that God wants me to abase myself; in all moments."

"I release the belief that God wants me to be contrite; in all moments."

"I release the belief that God wants me to be passive; in all moments."

"I release the belief that God wants me to be meek; in all moments."

"I recant my vow of martyrdom; in all moments."

"I recant my vow of poverty; in all moments."

"I recant my vow of humility; in all moments."

"I release confusing deficiency with loving God; in all moments."

"I release defining spirituality as having poverty; in all moments."

"I release the belief that money is evil; in all moments."

"I release the belief that happiness is a sin; in all moments."

"I release carrying the weight of the world on my shoulders; in all moments."

I shift my paradigm to joy, love, abundance, freedom, and wholeness; in all moments."

"I make space in this world for my personal joy, love, abundance, freedom and wholeness; in all moments."

"I remove all blockages to being centered in joy, love abundance, freedom and wholeness; in all moments."

"I stretch my capacity to accept joy, love, abundance, freedom and wholeness; in all moments."

In many past times, life was cruel and harsh. The only comfort may have come from believing that enduring the suffering endeared one to God. It was a great survival tool of the time. But it may be time to have another experience. I challenge everyone to challenge their own core beliefs to realize that they are still worthy of God's love even if they are rich beyond their wildest compare.

Free Your Spirit: Recant the Vows That Hinder Your Happiness

If you aren't attracting money, love, relationships, or kindnesses to yourself, it is not because you aren't worthy. God is not punishing you. You are not cursed. You are not born under a dark cloud. It is not your karma. God does NOT hate you.

In past lives we all did stints in different religious sects. In these lifetimes, we took oaths to refrain from earthly pleasures. We have taken vows of poverty, solitude, silence, etc. So if you are shy and have trouble speaking up, your issue could be as simple as this.

These are the initial taps I was given by my Spirit Guides to free humanity. When I started doing remote sessions, these issues were the first energy strands that I untangled in all my clients. Some of you still need to do them.

(Say each statement three times while tapping on your head and say it a fourth time while tapping on your chest.)

"I recant my vow of poverty; in all moments."

"I recant my vow of humility; in all moments."

"I recant my vow of silence; in all moments."

"I recant my vow of solitude; in all moments."

"I recant my vow of chastity; in all moments."

"I recant my vow of celibacy; in all moments."

"I recant my vow of servitude; in all moments."

"I recant my vow of martyrdom; in all moments."

"I recant my vow of self-deprecation; in all moments."

"I recant my vow of self-deprivation; in all moments."

"I recant my vow of obedience; in all moments."

"I recant my vow to be married only to God; in all moments."

"I recant all my vows to God; in all moments."

"I recant all self-defeating vows; in all moments."

"I recant my vows to all others; in all moments."

"I recant my vow to not transcend; in all moments."

Become a Millionaire

People have been asking for this. They have been praying for it as well. Please enjoy these taps as evidence that you are loved and heard. If you get to millionaire status before me, please consider investing in a Jenuine Healing Center. It will be a place where all can be uplifted by walking through its grounds. Godspeed.

(Say each statement three times while tapping on your head and say it a fourth time while tapping on your chest.)

"I am agreeable to wealth; in all moments."

"I resonate with wealth; in all moments."

"I release the fear of being wealthy; in all moments."

"I release the belief that being wealthy is overwhelming; in all moments."

"I release the belief that being wealthy means sacrificing my happiness; in all moments."

"I release the belief that being wealthy is too much work; in all moments."

"I release the belief that being wealthy is being spiritually bankrupt; in all moments."

"I release the belief that being wealthy is stressful; in all moments."

"I release the belief that being wealthy means selling out; in all moments."

"I release defining being wealthy as being selfish; in all moments."

"I release defining being wealthy as being spiritually unaware; in all moments."

"I release defining being wealthy as being evil; in all moments."

"I release defining being wealthy as sacrificing happiness; in all moments."

"I release defining being wealthy as being spiritually bankrupt; in all moments."

"I release the resistance to wealth; in all moments."

"I release the aversion to wealth; in all moments."

"I release the fear of wealth; in all moments."

"I release all limited beliefs about wealth; in all moments."

"I remove all negative programming regarding wealth; in all moments."

"I remove and dissolve all negative engrams regarding wealth; in all moments."

"I release being programmed to financially fail; in all moments."

"I remove all conscious and unconscious negative programming regarding wealth; in all moments."

"I infuse the sound frequency of my consciousness and subconscious to resonate with being a millionaire; in all moments."

"I imbue the light body of my consciousness and subconscious to emanate with being a millionaire; in all moments."

"Both my consciousness and subconscious resonate and emanate with being a millionaire; in all moments."

"I remove all negative correlations between my spiritual well being and wealth; in all moments."

"I remove all negative correlations between my mental well being and wealth; in all moments."

"I remove all negative correlations between my emotional well being and wealth; in all moments."

"I remove all negative correlations between my physical well being and wealth; in all moments."

"I reject all negative associations between my spiritual well being and wealth; in all moments."

"I reject all negative associations between my mental well being and wealth; in all moments."

"I reject all negative associations between my emotional well being and wealth; in all moments."

"I reject all negative associations between my physical well being and wealth; in all moments."

"I release all non-supportive beliefs about money; in all moments."

"I release all non-supportive opinions about money; in all moments."

"I release all non-supportive feelings about money; in all moments."

"I release all non-supportive experiences regarding money; in all moments."

"I shift my paradigm from believing negatively about money to believing that money is positive and uplifting; in all moments."

"I shift my paradigm from thinking negatively about money to thinking that money is positive and uplifting; in all moments."

"I shift my paradigm from feeling negatively about money to feeling that money is positive and uplifting; in all moments."

"I shift my paradigm from experiencing negativity about money to experiencing money as positive and uplifting; in all moments."

"I create a spiritual space to hold wealth; in all moments."

"I create a mental space to hold wealth; in all moments."

"I create an emotional space to hold wealth; in all moments."

"I create a physical space to hold wealth; in all moments."

"I remove all blockages to holding a spiritual space for wealth; in all moments."

"I remove all blockages to holding a mental space for wealth; in all moments."

"I remove all blockages to holding an emotional space for wealth; in all moments."

"I remove all blockages to holding a physical space for wealth; in all moments."

"I stretch my capacity to hold a spiritual space for wealth; in all moments."

"I stretch my capacity to hold a mental space for wealth; in all moments."

"I stretch my capacity to hold an emotional space for wealth; in all moments."

"I stretch my capacity to hold a physical space for wealth; in all moments."

"I align myself spiritually, mentally, emotionally and physically for wealth; in all moments."

"I resonate with a millionaire soul; in all moments."

"I resonate with a millionaire mind; in all moments."

"I resonate with a millionaire heart; in all moments."

"I resonate with a millionaire body; in all moments."

"My higher self creates a millionaire spiritual experience; in all moments."

"My higher self creates a millionaire mental experience; in all moments."

"My higher self creates a millionaire emotional experience; in all moments."

"My higher self creates a millionaire physical experience; in all moments."

"I am centered and empowered in spiritual wealth; in all moments."

"I am centered and empowered in mental wealth; in all moments."

"I am centered and empowered in emotional wealth; in all moments."

"I am centered, and empowered in physical wealth; in all moments."

"I am centered, aligned and empowered in spiritual, mental, emotional and physical wealth; in all moments."

"I am spiritually, mentally, emotionally and physically centered and empowered in being rich; in all moments."

"I empower all the world with my wealth; in all moments."

"I uplift humanity with my wealth; in all moments."

"I passionately and enthusiastically empower wealth in all others; in all moments."

"I graciously and enthusiastically receive wealth into my life; in all moments."

"I spiritually, mentally, emotionally and physically choose to get paid; in all moments."

"I spiritually, mentally, emotionally and physically graciously and enthusiastically accept payment; in all moments."

"My attention and awareness embrace wealth for all; in all moments."

"I release diminishing my self-worth and net worth; in all moments."

"I perpetuate an exponential self-worth and net worth; in all moments."

"My net worth is worth millions and my self-worth is priceless; in all moments."

"I am excellent at managing money; in all moments."

"I shift my paradigm from micromanaging the Universe to managing my own wealth in all moments."

"I release hating money; in all moments."

"I release being the enemy of money; in all moments."

"I release treating money like a stranger; in all moments."

"I release treating wealth as a foreign object; in all moments."

"I spiritually, mentally, emotionally and physically love money; in all moments."

"I am spiritually, mentally, emotionally and physically friends with money; in all moments."

"Money is spiritually, mentally, emotionally and physically devoted to me; in all moments."

"I am centered and empowered in my friendship of money; in all moments."

"My money perpetuates more money; in all moments."

"My money perpetuates my wealth; in all moments."

"Money is a seedbed for my millions; in all moments."

"My millions perpetuate the upliftment of humanity; in all moments."

"My millions are the seedbed for the wealth of humanity; in all moments."

"I am gracious and enthusiastic in continuously learning and gaining awareness; in all moments."

"I am wealthy in all ways; in all moments."

"I believe in being generous; in all moments."

"I have a generous mentality; in all moments."

"I have a generous heart; in all moments."

"I personify generosity; in all moments."

"I have a receptive soul; in all moments."

"I have a receptive mind; in all moments."

"I have a receptive heart; in all moments."

"I personify receptivity; in all moments."

"I have the essence of a millionaire; in all moments."

"I have a millionaire mind; in all moments."

"I have a millionaire heart; in all moments."

"I have a millionaire body; in all moments."

"I am the embodiment of being a millionaire; in all moments."

"I repair and fortify the financial wei chi of all my bodies; in all moments."

"I align all the spiritual, mental, emotional and physical financial aspects of myself; in all moments."

"I release and dissolve anything that does not support the divinity of my wealth; in all moments."

"I equivocate my wealth with joy, love, abundance, freedom and wholeness; in all moments."

"I am centered and empowered in being a millionaire; in all moments."

Buying Money

In a session, it came to me why so many people are in lack. Instead of using money to buy happiness they are using happiness to buy money. They are using all their abundance of joy, love, freedom and wholeness as currency to buy money.

People who spend all their time at a job that they don't like just for the pay are buying money. If people hate their job, they are using their love to buy money. If they are unhappy, they are using their joy to buy money. If they feel trapped in a job, they are using their freedom to buy money. If they feel pulled between their home life and their job, then they are buying money with their wholeness.

If this makes sense to you, these taps may help.

(Say each statement three times while tapping on your head and say it a fourth time while tapping on your chest.)

"I release selling my Joy to buy money; in all moments."

"I release selling my Love to buy money; in all moments."

"I release selling my Abundance to buy money; in all moments."

"I release selling my Freedom to buy money; in all moments."

"I release selling my Health to buy money; in all moments."

"I release selling my Success to buy money; in all moments."

"I release selling my Security to buy money; in all moments."

"I release selling my Companionship to buy money; in all moments."

"I release selling my Talent to buy money; in all moments."

"I release selling my Peace of mind to buy money; in all moments."

"I release selling my Wholeness to buy money; in all moments."

"I release selling my Life to buy money; in all moments."

"I release chasing money; in all moments."

"I shift my paradigm from chasing money to having Abundance; in all moments."

"I release buying money with my Joy; in all moments."

"I release buying money with my Love; in all moments."

"I release buying money with my Abundance; in all moments."

"I release buying money with my Freedom; in all moments."

"I release buying money with my Health; in all moments."

"I release buying money with my Success; in all moments."

"I release buying money with my Security; in all moments."

"I release buying money with my Companionship; in all moments."

"I release buying money with my Talent; in all moments."

"I release buying money with my Peace of mind; in all moments."

"I release buying money with my Wholeness; in all moments."

"I release buying money with my Life; in all moments."

"I shift my paradigm from buying money to having Abundance; in all moments."

"I am centered in Joy, Love, Abundance, Freedom, Health, Success, Security, Companionship, Peace, Life and Wholeness; in all moments."

It may seem like we have to do what we have to do to make money. But for so many, it doesn't seem worth it. Maybe these taps will free people from a habitual belief system that is selling them short.

Chasing Monetary Wealth

There is a spiritual law called the law of reversed efforts. It states that the harder you try to have something, the further away it will be.

Also, the reason that the taps include doing them as a surrogate for humanity is because it is a way to overreach on an intention. By broadening the scope of the intention, it makes the *individual* intention more able to manifest. Also, it creates a portal for manifestation to wish good intention for others.

(Say each statement three times while tapping on your head and say it a fourth time while tapping on your chest.)

"I declare myself a surrogate for humanity in doing these taps; in all moments."

"I release being enslaved to monetary wealth; in all moments."

"I remove all glass ceilings that chasing monetary wealth put on me; in all moments."

"I release being at the mercy of monetary wealth; in all moments."

"I release diminishing myself in the pursuit of monetary wealth; in all moments."

"I bow out of all ventures that don't serve my best interests; in all moments."

"I release being duped by the desire for monetary wealth; in all moments."

Embrace the Good Stuff!

There are social conditionings and muscle memory that refuse the good things that life has to offer. We were brainwashed into believing that it is a pious thing to go without. The brain filters out at least eighty percent of what it feels is not relevant. Here is to making the good things in life relevant again.

(Say each statement three times while tapping on your head and say it a fourth time while tapping on your chest.)

"I release filtering out the joy; in all moments."

"I release filtering out the love; in all moments."

"I release filtering out abundance; in all moments."

"I release filtering out freedom; in all moments."

"I release filtering out health; in all moments."

"I release filtering out empowerment; in all moments."

"I release making joy in my life irrelevant; in all moments."

"I release making love in my life irrelevant; in all moments."

"I release making abundance in my life irrelevant; in all moments."

"I release making freedom in my life irrelevant; in all moments."

"I release making health in my life irrelevant; in all moments."

"I release making empowerment in my life irrelevant; in all moments."

"I reintegrate joy into every cell of my beingness; in all moments."

"I reintegrate love into every cell of my beingness; in all moments."

"I reintegrate abundance into every cell of my beingness; in all moments."

"I reintegrate freedom into every cell of my beingness; in all moments."

"I reintegrate optimal health into every cell of my beingness; in all moments."

"I reintegrate empowerment into every cell of my beingness; in all moments."

"I reintegrate joy into every cell of my conscious awareness; in all moments."

"I reintegrate love into every cell of my conscious awareness; in all moments."

"I reintegrate abundance into every cell of my conscious awareness; in all moments."

"I reintegrate freedom into every cell of my conscious awareness; in all moments."

"I reintegrate optimal health into every cell of my conscious awareness; in all moments."

"I reintegrate empowerment into every cell of my conscious awareness; in all moments."

"I exist, operate, and breathe Joy, Love, Abundance, Freedom, Health and Wholeness; in all moments.

Honoring Abundance

An affluent friend once told me the secret to being rich. It is to be grateful for every penny and to not judge it as being too inconsequential to be valued. You know the stereotype of the rich old man pinching every penny? He isn't pinching it. He is giving it reverence as a symbol of his wealth still flowing to him. He is paying homage to his abundance.

Just like many of us dismiss the pennies, we also dismiss our affluence in other areas as well. For instance, billions of people around the world have never sat in a tub of clean, fresh water and been able to wash themselves clean. Billions have never had a room assigned just for their items and their personal comfort and privacy. Billions of people have never walked under trees and been able to hear the rustling of leaves in the breeze. These are all priceless experiences that many of us partake in with no thought or fear of not having them.

Billions of people are not able to walk into a grocery store and choose any fresh, clean item that they crave in the moment. Multitudes have to struggle for every meal they eat, that is, if they are able to eat anything at all. Billions of people are denied the right to learn, know, make decisions and participate in conversations about the things that affect them.

When someone points these things out to another, it is in a chiding way that creates defensiveness in the receiver. That is not the point. The point is to be happy! Celebrate your good fortune.

Be grateful to whatever God you choose for the good fortune. Pinch those experiences. They are evidence of your good fortune, and they perpetuate abundant living.

The banking system and the conditioning of how to engage money is the antithesis to the spiritual law of abundance. The reason so many people are without money is because they are working counter to spiritual law.

Money is not evil. This was a concept ingrained in the impoverished so they could tolerate their stance of lack. They were taught that they were special because they did not succumb to the "evils" of wealth, and that they were nobler. The rich enjoyed such quaint musings because it meant that fewer poor people would grab at their wealth. It was a great symbiotic relationship between the rich and the lacking.

But the spiritual law of abundance states that all are worthy of abundance. It doesn't necessarily have to be monetary abundance but money is a component of it. Money has a neutral charge, meaning it is neither positive or negative. It is only given the charge that we give it.

Money should, and can, flow as effortlessly as a river of pure water. What we are taught about stuffing all our abundance into a bank is counter to the spiritual law of abundance, which mandates its steady flow. Hoarding money is as limiting as hoarding water. A stored pool of water will stagnate and breed terrible disease and so will stored money. Philanthropists understand this concept and work with the natural flow of giving.

The churches of old understood this process and so tithing was a way to keep monetary abundance flowing. But once something is mandated, it no longer flows willingly and effortlessly. It stagnates in pools this way and is acerbated when the process is met with resentment.

A way to gain a better understanding of abundance is by using the analogy of water. Abundance can, and does, flow as easily as water for those who do not focus on hoarding it. Give abundance easily and more will flow to you. Let it pass through your hands and use what you need. Always trust that there will be enough.

Never lend money. If it can't be given as a gift, it shouldn't be given at all. If you give it out freely, the Universe will send it back to you in some way. So if you are going to lend money, lend it to the Universe. It is the only reliable source for repayment. There is no value in extending your energy out and having it anchored to another. The only value is in learning that this is never a scenario that you want to agree to again.

Honor abundance by accepting it into your life in a multitude of ways just like water comes pouring, flowing or is piped into your life. Do not begrudge anyone else the flow of abundance. See it as a natural state to ebb, flow, evaporate and descend. One should observe with as much interest and gratitude as one watches the rain clouds empty on a dry day. This stance is more in accordance with spiritual law.

(Say each statement three times while tapping on your head and say it a fourth time while tapping on your chest.)

"I release needing money; in all moments."

"I release asking for money; in all moments."

"I release the need to search for money; in all moments."

"I release the fear of ending the search for money; in all moments."

"I release confusing ending the search for money with poverty; in all moments."

"I release being driven to make money; in all moments."

"I release kowtowing to those with money; in all moments."

"I release distancing myself from my own abundance; in all moments."

"I release trapping myself in unworthiness; in all moments."

"I remove all filters of fear of being without; in all moments."

"I remove all filters of poverty; in all moments."

"I remove all filters of a self-defeating ego; in all moments."

"I remove all filters of deference to others with money; in all moments."

"I release the fear of trusting; in all moments."

"I release the fear of having; in all moments."

"I release confusing new consciousness for old consciousness; in all moments."

"I remove all engrams of old consciousness; in all moments."

"I release confusing expanding my abundance with fear of losing it again; in all moments."

"I release the fear of bleeding out; in all moments."

"I release confusing spending money with bleeding out; in all moments."

"I remove all linear filters regarding abundance; in all moments."

"I connect to all hearts through abundance; in all moments."

"I dissolve all fear filters with my abundance; in all moments."

"I dissolve all ego filters with my abundance; in all moments."

"I beckon all Souls back to love with my generous spirit; in all moments."

"I send all energy matrices into the light and sound that cause poverty or depravity; in all moments."

"I command all complex energy matrices that cause poverty or depravity to be escorted into the light and sound; in all moments."

"I send all energy matrices into the light and sound that are not lovingly serving abundance; in all moments."

"I command all complex energy matrices that are not lovingly serving abundance to be escorted into the light and sound; in all moments."

Learn to Receive

It is Abundance to wake knowing that you will have food to eat that day.

It is Abundance to have a land that you can call home.

It is Abundance to have your own room with your own bed and your own door that you can shut and lock at will.

It is Abundance to choose any vocation, any school and anywhere to live and work to manifest your purpose.

It is Abundance to draw a tub of clean fresh water to soak in and then empty.

Some people are great givers but they aren't very good at receiving. This robs others of the joy of giving. This is a great time of the year to change that. Here are some taps to assist with this issue:

(Say each statement three times while tapping on your head and say it a fourth time while tapping on your chest.)

"I release the aversion to receiving; in all moments."

"I release being a martyr; in all moments."

"I release viewing gift giving as competition; in all moments."

"I release feeling unworthy to receive; in all moments."

"I release viewing gift exchange as manipulation; in all moments."

"I release denying the receiver; in all moments."

"I release interrupting the fluidity of exchange; in all moments."

"I release denying a gift to feel superior; in all moments."

"I accept the ebb and flow of receiving and giving; in all moments."

"I am centered in giving and receiving; in all moments."

Liberty and Abundance for All

Anybody who is tired of the status quo, wants to be wealthy, feels discouraged with the state of affairs, wants to make a difference, takes up causes, cares about the survival of other species, quietly subscribes to conspiracy theories, believes we can do better, wants to see change, or is just bored and indifferent, needs to do these taps.

(Say each statement three times while tapping on your head and say it a fourth time while tapping on your chest.)

"I release being enslaved to the warlords of the wealthy; in all moments."

"I release humanity being enslaved to the warlords of the wealthy; in all moments."

"I release being shackled to the warlords of the wealthy; in all moments."

"I release humanity being shackled to the warlords of the wealthy;

in all moments."

"I release engaging the warlords of the wealthy; in all moments."

"I release humanity engaging the warlords of the wealthy; in all moments."

"I recant all vows and agreements between myself and the warlords of the wealthy; in all moments."

"I recant all vows and agreements between humanity and the warlords of the wealthy; in all moments."

"I remove all curses between myself and the warlords of the wealthy; in all moments."

"I remove all curses between humanity and the warlords of the wealthy; in all moments."

"I remove all blessings between myself and the warlords of the wealthy; in all moments."

"I remove all blessings between humanity and the warlords of the wealthy; in all moments."

"I sever all strings and cords between myself and the warlords of the wealthy; in all moments."

"I sever all strings and cords between humanity and the warlords of the wealthy; in all moments."

"I dissolve all karmic ties between myself and the warlords of the wealthy; in all moments."

"I dissolve all karmic ties between humanity and the warlords of the wealthy; in all moments."

"I remove all shackles of the warlords of the wealthy from myself; in all moments."

"Humanity removes all shackles of the warlords from itself; in all moments."

"I remove all the implants that the warlords of the wealthy have embedded in me; in all moments."

"Humanity removes all the implants that the warlords of the wealthy have embedded within it; in all moments."

"I crumble all the archaic structures of the warlords of the wealthy; in all moments."

"Humanity crumbles all the archaic structures of the warlords of the wealthy; in all moments."

"I take back and restore my keystone from the warlords of the wealthy; in all moments."

"Humanity takes back and restores its keystone from the warlords of the wealthy; in all moments."

"The first rule of the warlords of the wealthy is eliminated; in all moments."

"The first rule of the warlords of the wealthy in regard to humanity is eliminated; in all moments."

"I remove all the pain, burden, limitations and engrams that the warlords of the wealthy have put on me; in all moments."

"Humanity removes all the pain, burden, limitations and engrams that the warlords of the wealthy have put on it; in all moments."

"I remove all the pain, burden, limitations and engrams that I have put on all others due to the warlords of the wealthy; in all moments."

"Humanity removes all the pain, burden, limitations and engrams that it has put on all others due to the warlords of the wealthy; in all moments."

"I take back all the joy, love, abundance, freedom, health, success, security, companionship, creativity, peace, life, wholeness, beauty, enthusiasm, contentment, spirituality, enlightenment, confidence, family, intellect and the ability to discern that the warlords of the wealthy have taken from me; in all moments."

"Humanity takes back all the joy, love, abundance, freedom, health, success, security, companionship, creativity, peace, life, wholeness, beauty, enthusiasm, contentment, spirituality, enlightenment, confidence, family, intellect and the ability to discern that the warlords of the wealthy have taken from it; in all moments."

"I give back to all others all the joy, love, abundance, freedom, health, success, security, companionship, creativity, peace, life, wholeness, beauty, enthusiasm, contentment, spirituality, enlightenment, confidence, family, intellect and the ability to discern that I have been taken from them due to the warlords of the wealthy; in all moments."

"Humanity gives back to all others all the joy, love, abundance, freedom, health, success, security, companionship, creativity, peace, life, wholeness, beauty, enthusiasm, contentment, spirituality, enlightenment, confidence, family, intellect and the ability to discern that they have taken from all others due to the warlords of the wealthy; in all moments."

"I release resonating with the warlords of the wealthy; in all moments."

"Humanity releases resonating with the warlords of the wealthy; in all moments."

"I release emanating with the warlords of the wealthy; in all moments."

"Humanity releases emanating with the warlords of the wealthy; in all moments."

"I extract all of the warlords of the wealthy from my sound frequency; in all moments."

"I extract all of the warlords of the wealthy from Humanity's sound frequency; in all moments."

"I extract all of the warlords of the wealthy from my light emanation; in all moments."

"I extract all of the warlords of the wealthy from Humanity's light emanation; in all moments."

"I shift my paradigm from the warlords of the wealthy to joy, love, abundance, freedom, health, success, security, companionship, creativity, peace, life, wholeness, beauty, enthusiasm, contentment, spirituality, enlightenment, confidence, family, intellect and the ability to discern; in all moments."

"I shift Humanity's paradigm from the warlords of the wealthy to joy, love, abundance, freedom, health, success, security, companionship, creativity, peace, life, wholeness, beauty, enthusiasm, contentment, spirituality, enlightenment, confidence, family, intellect and the ability to discern; in all moments."

"I transcend the warlords of the wealthy; in all moments."

"Humanity transcends the warlords of the wealthy; in all moments."

"I strip all the illusion off of the warlords of the wealthy; in all moments."

"Humanity strips all of the illusion off of the warlords of the wealthy; in all moments."

"I repair and fortify the wei chi of all my bodies; in all moments."

"Humanity repairs and fortifies the wei chi of all its layers; in all moments."

"I remove all masks, walls and armor off of the warlords of the wealthy; in all moments."

"Humanity removes all masks, walls and armor off of the warlords of the wealthy; in all moments."

"I am centered and empowered in divine love; in all moments."

"Humanity is centered and empowered in divine love; in all moments."

"I and Humanity are aligned with truth; in all moments."

"I and Humanity resonate and emanate joy, love, abundance and freedom; in all moments."

Living Your Abundance

Abundance is a 360-degree perception. Monetary abundance is one notch on the dial. Everyone in society is being trained to fixate on that one notch. It is no different than everyone being fixated on the time waiting for the clock to strike noon. It negates all the other minutes just waiting for that one time to be struck.

That is exactly what people do with monetary abundance. They negate all other forms of abundance. Just like the watched clock never changes, it seems to be that way with monetary windfall as well. But when one removes their fixation on time or monetary wealth, both goals are met effortlessly. Time flies and abundance flows.

(Say each statement three times out loud while continuously tapping on the top of your head at the crown chakra and say it a fourth time while tapping on your chest.)

"I release the fear of living my Abundance; in all moments."

"I release allowing outer circumstances to interfere with me living my Abundance; in all moments."

"I release being overwhelmed by the thought of living my

Abundance; in all moments."

"I release defining living my Abundance with massive responsibility; in all moments."

"I release defining living my Abundance as a burden; in all moments."

"I release allowing unworthiness to sabotage living my Abundance; in all moments."

"I release all the confusion surrounding accepting my Abundance; in all moments."

"I release allowing someone else to define Abundance for me; in all moments."

"I release allowing anyone to dictate or micromanage my Abundance; in all moments."

"I release losing touch with my Abundance; in all moments."

"I make space in this world to live my Abundance; in all moments."

"I remove all blockages to living my Abundance; in all moments."

"I connect wholeheartedly in living my Abundance; in all moments."

"I stretch my capacity to live my Abundance; in all moments."

"I release any fear, doubt and hesitancy in living my Abundance; in all moments."

"I now recognize how to live my Abundance; in all moments."

"I am centered and empowered in living my Abundance; in all moments."

"I resonate and emanate with living my Abundance; in all moments."

Manifesting Abundance

The trick to having the taps work faster for you is, after you do the taps, don't talk about all the reasons you felt compelled to do the taps. So after you do these taps on abundance, don't talk about the late bills or how broke you are.

It creates a fertile environment to receive if you adopt a state of expectation and gratitude. This opens your energy to receive.

(Say each statement three times while tapping on your head and say it a fourth time while tapping on your chest.)

"I make space in this world to manifest perpetual, monetary abundance; in all moments."

"I remove all blockages to manifesting perpetual, monetary abundance; in all moments."

"I open all portals to manifesting perpetual, monetary abundance; in all moments."

"I stretch my capacity to manifest perpetual, monetary abundance; in all moments."

"I am centered and empowered in manifesting perpetual, monetary abundance; in all moments."

"I resonate, emanate, and am interconnected to all life in manifesting perpetual, monetary abundance; in all moments."

Opening up the Floodgates of Abundance

We are all tiny spigots in the waterfall of life. What we do or don't do doesn't seem to matter in the grand scheme of things. But it does. Too many of us have shut down our flow. It happened out of an inability to share our gifts, being so tired of trying, hearing we don't matter or not having anyone to love us back.

Humanity needs your spigot turned on full blast. You matter. Your flow matters. Turning your spigot on encourages others to turn theirs on. It could open their flow by osmosis. It is no matter how it happens only that it does. Life needs to flow again. Love needs that perpetual flow. You are important in making that happen.

It doesn't matter what shut you down. We all have a story about someone refusing our love, someone hurting us, someone denying us the right to love. This is the nature of the world that fortifies our indignation at not accepting our love. But that is the illusion. The multitudes are waiting for your love.

If you have no one to love you, love others more. There are those in the world who are so depraved of love that they hurt and destroy others to cope. How does the world deal with that? How does one not feel helpless? The helplessness is what they are feeling in their depravity. It is a reaction to the lack of love.

Every single person is empowered in their capacity to love. When we all refuse the stark reality of the universal thirst and give all that we have regardless of how much we get to drink, we practice unconditional love. It touches upon the divine. Open your own floodgates; let the process satiate your thirst. Refuse to judge anyone. Refuse to deem anyone less worthy. Encourage them to share all that they are.

There is one way that man has cut off himself from nature. Nature continues to give and give no matter what is done to it. Man has developed the superiority to withhold his gifts. This is man's own demise. He must return to nature and do as the female does. A woman knows how to love under every circumstance. It is her nature.

That need to defend yourself, that need to be right, that need to keep your composure is what a closed spigot feels like. Surrendering, feeling vulnerable, saying "I am sorry" and meaning it are the experiences of the open heart. Do it more. Do it often. Do it so others can know the freedom of it from observing you.

When we are all open and pour our love into the world for everyone to partake of, we reopen the universal waterfall one drop, one trickle, one stream at a time. What can you do to open up the floodgates? Who can you open up right now in your day? How can you serve someone else with your kindness, a good word, some encouragement?

Humanity thriving depends on this process happening within all of us. Make it a project to open up the rustiest pipelines. You can do this. This is your task. This is the greatest thing you can do for humanity. If you have no one to love, figure it out. Feed your love to a hungry world by doing something as simple as loving the birds or sharing a kindness. Go beyond your comfort zone a little bit more each time.

There are many people all over the world who are being loving and kind in their own shy way. Let's do what we can to make it the norm. Love beyond all reason, discernment and any limited capacity. This is how we connect to our own greatness. This is how we make this life count more. I support all in this purpose. I will be loving right by your side and encouraging the floodgates to open. In this way, we are all powerful beyond compare. Amazing you, amazing me, amazing we.

If we can open our floodgate to love, we can also open our floodgate to abundance.

Release Crying Poor

(Say each statement three times out loud while tapping on the top of your head at the crown chakra and say it a fourth time while tapping on your chest.)

"I release the belief that it is noble to be poor; in all moments."

"I release subscribing to only one kind of wealth; in all moments."

"I release converting my other forms of wealth into monetary gain; in all moments."

"I release having such a high conversion rate for monetary rate; in all moments."

"I release crying poor to get special treatment; in all moments."

"I release being a martyr in money issues; in all moments."

"I release being uncomfortable with wealth; in all moments."

"I release thinking of money as evil; in all moments."

"I release confusing monetary wealth with responsibility; in all moments."

"I release believing that I must be poor; in all moments."

"I release telling people that I am poor; in all moments."

"I release an aversion to wealth; in all moments."

"I recant all vows of poverty and unworthiness; in all moments."

"I release the belief that spirituality is the polarized opposite of wealth; in all moments."

"I remove all limiting engrams including all those of lack; in all moments."

"I claim both my goodness and my wealth; in all moments."

"I shift my paradigm from *have not* to *have*; in all moments."

"I claim my birthright of joy, love, abundance and freedom; in all moments."

"I am centered and abundant in my own empowerment of wealth; in all moments."

"I resonate and emanate wealth; in all moments."

Release Limiting Concepts of Money

The concept of money exists on the mental realm. It is matter of digging deeper to release this artificial concept of self-worth from our repertoire. Beyond this concept lies spiritual freedom. Money itself is just a tool that is used to benefit the individual. Money is only harmful if used as a weapon.

But the concept of money has an identity of its own. It has been so twisted and bastardized to bend the will of innocence that it taints all who look upon it too long with power and corruption. Being free of the concept of money frees humanity up for spiritual freedom. In a way, it is like a precursor.

Please do not fear the collapse of the fall of money. It is a hideous dragon that has doused itself in comeliness. Rejoice with all the heavens at its demise. The spiritual adepts have been working towards this goal to release the shackles from innocence for so long.

Pour love and gratitude into the false wounds that the illusion of lack of money has created. Love is your balm. You are, and always have been, whole.

(Say each statement three times while tapping on your head and say it a fourth time while tapping on your chest.)

"I declare myself a surrogate for humanity in doing these taps; in all moments."

"I release worshiping the concept of money; in all moments."

"I release the fear of losing the concept of money; in all moments."

"I release basing my self-worth against the backdrop of the concept of money; in all moments."

"I release converting the joy of the moment into worry over money; in all moments."

"I release equivocating the concept of money with survival; in all moments."

"I release confusing the concept of money for God; in all moments."

"I release calculating my happiness in relationship to the concept of money; in all moments."

"I release siphoning off all my essence and pouring it into the concept of money; in all moments."

"I release using up all my good intentions with concerns over the concept of money; in all moments."

"I release being enslaved to the concept of money; in all moments."

"I remove all vivaxes between myself and the concept of money; in all moments."

"I remove all tentacles between myself and the concept of money; in all moments."

"I remove all engrams that the concept of money has put on me; in all moments."

"I send all energy matrices into the light and sound that convince me I need money; in all moments."

"I send all energy matrices into the light and sound that distract me from my essence with the concept of money; in all moments."

"I strip all illusion off of the concept of money; in all moments."

"I remove all masks, walls, and armor off of the concept of money; in all moments."

"I withdraw all of my energy from the concept of money; in all moments."

"I remove all vivaxes between myself and need; in all moments."

"I remove associating the concept of money with need; in all moments."

"I remove all tentacles between myself and need; in all moments."

"I remove all engrams that need has put on me; in all moments."

"I send all energy matrices into the light and sound that immerse me in need; in all moments."

"I recant all vows and agreements between myself and the concept of money; in all moments."

"I remove all curses between myself and the concept of money; in all moments."

"I remove all blessings between myself and the concept of money; in all moments."

"I release spending my days chasing money; in all moments."

"I sever all strings and cords between myself and money; in all moments."

"I dissolve all karmic ties between myself and money; in all moments."

"I remove all the pain, burden, limitations, and illusion of separateness that the concept of money has put on me; in all moments."

"I remove all the pain, burden, limitations, and illusion of separateness that the concept of money has caused me to put on others; in all moments."

"I take back all the good that the concept of money has taken from me; in all moments."

"I give back to others all the good that the concept of money has caused me to take from them; in all moments."

"I release resonating with the concept of money; in all moments."

"I release emanating with the concept of money; in all moments."

"I extract all of the concept of money from my sound frequency; in all moments."

"I extract all of the concept of money from my light emanation; in all moments."

"I extract all of the concept of money from the Universal sound frequency; in all moments."

"I extract all of the concept of money from the Universal light emanation; in all moments."

"I shift my paradigm from the concept of money to spiritual freedom; in all moments."

"I shift the Universal paradigm from the concept of money to spiritual freedom; in all moments."

"I am centered and empowered in spiritual freedom; in all moments."

"I am centered and empowered in Universal spiritual freedom; in all moments."

"I resonate and emanate spiritual freedom; in all moments."

"The Universe resonates and emanates spiritual freedom for all; in all moments."

Eradicating Poverty for All

These taps are done as a surrogate for humanity. It is much easier to manifest for yourself if you outflow your intentions to assist others. Your benevolence is an intention that you can control without depleting yourself. Offering benevolence to others is a form of priming the pump for your own abundance.

(Say each statement three times while tapping on your head and say it a fourth time while tapping on your chest.)

"We declare ourselves surrogates for humanity in doing these taps; in all moments."

"We snuff out poverty; in all moments."

"We release being entrenched in poverty; in all moments."

"We release being seduced into poverty by fear; in all moments."

"We release being subjugated by poverty; in all moments."

"We release being converted to poverty; in all moments."

"We release being rendered ineffective by poverty; in all moments."

"We release being isolated by poverty; in all moments."

"We release conceding to poverty; in all moments."

"We release being paralyzed by poverty; in all moments."

"We release wasting our energy in poverty; in all moments."

"We release being manipulated into poverty; in all moments."

"We release being defamed by poverty; in all moments."

"We release being demonized by poverty; in all moments."

"We release being scattered to the wind by poverty; in all moments."

"We remove all vivaxes between ourselves and poverty; in all moments."

"We remove all tentacles between ourselves and poverty; in all moments."

"We remove the claws of poverty from our beingness; in all moments."

"We remove all programming and conditioning that poverty has put on us; in all moments."

"We remove all engrams that poverty has put on us; in all moments."

"We release giving up our sovereignty to poverty; in all moments."

"We release attacking abundance for poverty; in all moments."

"We strip all illusion off of poverty; in all moments."

"We withdraw all our energy from poverty; in all moments."

"We remove all masks, walls, and armor from poverty; in all moments."

"We heal the impoverished; in all moments."

"We send all energy matrices of poverty into the light and sound; in all moments."

"We render poverty helpless; in all moments."

"We command all complex energy matrices of poverty to be escorted into the light and sound; in all moments."

"We release being separated from our purpose by poverty; in all moments."

"We release being verbally assaulted by poverty; in all moments."

"We release confusing poverty for abundance; in all moments."

"We release being seduced by poverty; in all moments."

"We release being deaf, mute, blind or ignorant to poverty; in all moments."

"We nullify all contracts between ourselves and poverty; in all moments."

"We remove all blind spots in regards to poverty; in all moments."

"We recant all vows and agreements between ourselves and poverty; in all moments."

"We remove all curses between ourselves and poverty; in all moments."

"We remove all blessings between ourselves and poverty; in all moments."

"We sever all strings, cords and wires between ourselves and poverty; in all moments."

"We dissolve all karmic ties between ourselves and poverty; in all moments."

"We remove all the pain, burden and limitations that poverty has put on us; in all moments."

"We remove all the pain, burden and limitations that we have put on all others due to poverty; in all moments."

"We remove all shackles that poverty has put on us; in all moments."

"We remove ourselves from all prisons that poverty has put us in;

in all moments."

"We remove all the fear, futility, and unworthiness that poverty has put on us; in all moments."

"We remove all the fear, futility, and unworthiness that we have put on all others due to poverty; in all moments."

"We remove all the self-righteousness, entitlement, and anger that poverty has put on us; in all moments."

"We remove all the self-righteousness, entitlement, and anger that we have put on all others due to poverty; in all moments."

"We remove all the apathy, indifference, and illusion of separateness that poverty has put on us; in all moments."

"We remove all the apathy, indifference, and illusion of separateness that we have put on all others due to poverty; in all moments."

"We take back ALL that poverty has taken from us; in all moments."

"We give back to all others ALL that we have taken from them; in all moments."

"We release resonating with poverty; in all moments."

"We release emanating with poverty; in all moments."

"We extract all poverty from our sound frequency and the universal sound frequency; in all moments."

"We extract all poverty from our light emanation and the universal light emanation; in all moments."

"We take back our empowerment; in all moments."

"We shift the universal paradigm from poverty to abundance; in all moments."

"We universally transcend poverty; in all moments."

"We are universally centered and empowerment in Divine abundance; in all moments."

"We universally resonate, emanate, and are interconnected in Divine abundance; in all moments."

"We eradicate poverty consciousness; in all moments."

"We eradicate systemic poverty; in all moments."

"We eradicate milking individuals into poverty; in all moments."

Stop Chasing Money

I facilitated a session with someone who was very concerned about having money. There was no financial struggle but the issue of money was always in the forefront. She sabotaged relationships if the suitor wasn't affluent. She deferred to her parents way into her adulthood because they were rich. Happiness was elusive.

In her session, it became clear that there was no separation made between happiness and money. She thought of them as one and the same. She did not think it was possible to have happiness without money, but I made her look at the situation more closely. She did know rich people who weren't happy, so the words did NOT mean the same thing. She had chosen money over relationships. Yet that did not make her happy either.

Happiness and money may be on parallel paths sometimes, but that doesn't mean they are synonymous. I brought up the analogy of owning a dog. If your dog doesn't come to you and you chase after it, it will keep running away. This was similar to her relationship with money. She was chasing it and it was running away.

If you want to get your dog back, you walk in the other direction so it happily follows you. She needed to walk away from money towards happiness and trust that the comfortable finances would follow. The same thing could be true of happiness. If one chases it, it may be elusive. But if one just walks the path, it will walk right by their side.

Here are some taps to assist if this issue resonates for you:

(Say each statement three times while tapping on your head and say it a fourth time while tapping on your chest.)

"I release the belief that money is happiness; in all moments."

"I release chasing money; in all moments."

"I release choosing money over happiness; in all moments."

"I release being enslaved by money; in all moments."

"I release the belief that being poor equals happiness; in all moments."

"I release the belief that money and happiness are at cross purposes; in all moments."

"I release the belief that money is the only form of wealth; in all moments."

"I release negating my own abundance; in all moments."

"I shift my paradigm to happiness and abundance; in all moments."

"I am centered in happiness and abundance; in all moments."

Stop Limiting Abundance

The problem with thinking that money is the only form of abundance is that some people measure their own worth by it. There are so many other ways that we are shown how much we are valued:

- by how many smiles we illicit,
- the safety and sanctity of our home,
- the increments of love that we receive,
- the amount of beauty that we can recognize and take in,
- the continuous free training we are given in life's lessons

The love and gratitude we are shown is endless and is only limited by how much we can take in and appreciate.

(Say this statement three times out loud while continuously tapping on the top of your head at the crown chakra and say it a fourth time while tapping on your head.)

"I release coagulating abundance to the coarsest vibration; in all moments."

"I release putting limitations on abundance; in all moments."

"I extract all opinions, arrogance or judgment from abundance; in all moments."

"I release micromanaging how I attract or assimilate abundance; in all moments."

"I release trying to hoard abundance; in all moments."

"I release making abundance a competition; in all moments."

"I release needing abundance to be proved to me; in all moments."

"I remove all the conditions that I have put on abundance; in all moments."

"I transform abundance into a fluidity through kind acts and sharing; in all moments."

"I expound abundance everywhere; in all moments."

"I transform everything into abundance; in all moments."

"I transform abundance into an all-permeating factor through Gratitude and Grace; in all moments."

"I breathe abundance into my universal existence through Gratitude and Grace; in all moments."

"I am imbued with the Gratitude and Grace of an all permeating abundance; in all moments."

Tapping into Money

There are different reasons that people push money away. It was usually set up in a past life when they didn't have abundance and so they cursed the rich who were undoubtedly indifferent to the poor. The problem with cursing the wealthy is that all curses come home. If you cursed the wealthy in a past life, how could you accept wealth in this life? You would also be accepting all the curses that you know you have put on the wealthy. This is what we deal with in encompassing our whole self.

As it is now, people have been inadvertently avoiding being wealthy to avoid the curses they know they put on those with money. Instead of doing that, just remove the curses. This is the subtle dynamics at play in freeing yourself to be able to accept having money.

Some issues in regards to not having money are primal. Below are some taps to free your dynamics with money from the limitations you put on it.

(Say each statement three times out loud while continuously tapping on the top of your head at the crown chakra and say it a fourth time while tapping on your chest.)

"I release basing my worth on making money; in all moments."

"I release using making money to validate my existence; in all moments."

"I release the belief that making money is the answer to all problems; in all moments."

"I release obsessing over making money; in all moments."

"I release equivocating making money with self-love; in all moments."

"I release using making money as a contingency to loving myself; in all moments."

"I release using making money to prove my importance; in all moments."

"I release pushing money away through desire; in all moments."

"I release pushing money away by trying to make it; in all moments."

"I release the belief that I am incapable of making money; in all moments."

"I release being beaten down by the process of making money; in all moments."

"I release confusing the ability to make money with having abundance; in all moments."

"I release the belief that making money is a natural process; in all moments."

"I release coming out of my center to make money; in all moments."

"I release dissipating my energy trying to make money; in all moments."

"I release pushing money away by trying to generate it; in all moments."

"I release the belief that money is the answer to all my problems; in all moments."

"I release sabotaging monetary abundance with making money; in all moments."

"I release sabotaging monetary abundance with not making money; in all moments."

"I released being enslaved to the process of making money; in all moments."

"I released being enslaved to not making money; in all moments."

"I recant all vows and agreements between myself and making money; in all moments."

"I recant all vows and agreements between myself and not making money; in all moments."

"I remove all curses between myself and making money; in all moments."

"I remove all curses between myself and not making money; in all moments."

"I remove all blessings between myself and making money; in all moments."

"I remove all blessings between myself and not making money; in all moments."

"I sever all strings and cords between myself and making money; in all moments."

"I sever all strings and cords between myself and not making money; in all moments."

"I dissolve all karmic ties between myself and making money; in all moments."

"I dissolve all karmic ties between myself and not making money; in all moments."

"I release punishing myself by not making money; in all moments."

"I release using not making money as a scapegoat; in all moments."

"I withdraw all my energy from making money; in all moments."

"I withdraw all my energy from not making money; in all moments."

"I release resonating with making money; in all moments."

"I release resonating with not making money; in all moments."

"I release emanating with making money; in all moments."

"I release emanating with not making money; in all moments."

"I extract all of making money from my sound frequency; in all moments."

"I extract all of not making money from my sound frequency; in all moments."

"I extract all of making money from my light emanation; in all moments."

"I extract all of not making money from my light emanation; in all moments."

"I shift my paradigm from making money to joy, love, abundance, freedom, health, success, security, companionship, creativity, peace, life, wholeness, beauty, enthusiasm, contentment, spirituality, enlightenment, confidence, family, intelligence and the ability to discern; in all moments."

"I shift my paradigm from not making money to joy, love, abundance, freedom, health, success, security, companionship, creativity, peace, life, wholeness, beauty, enthusiasm, contentment, spirituality, enlightenment, confidence, family, intelligence and the ability to discern; in all moments."

"I transcend making money; in all moments."

"I transcend not making money; in all moments."

"I release allowing an outside source to dictate my monetary abundance; in all moments."

"I release allowing the past to dictate my monetary abundance; in all moments."

"I release sabotaging my monetary abundance; in all moments."

"I release allowing any aspect of my internal dialogue to diminish my monetary abundance; in all moments."

"I shift my paradigm from making money to monetary abundance; in all moments."

"I shift my paradigm from not making money to monetary abundance; in all moments."

"I release micromanaging the process of monetary abundance; in all moments."

"I am centered and empowered in monetary abundance; in all moments."

"I resonate and emanate monetary abundance; in all moments."

Transform Dark Money

There are so many people who want money. They believe they need it to move forward. But money has a negative charge right now and perhaps if they had money, they would be susceptible to the vibrations that it now carries. A good way to remedy that is to raise the vibration on money itself and strip off the negativity of the charge it may presently carry.

Having money should be as innocent as having a bargaining tool with the neighbor. Everything of power, corruption and diminishing others must go.

(Say each statement three times while tapping on your head and say if a fourth time while tapping on your chest.)

"We release the manipulative powers of money; in all moments."

"We release pandering to money; in all moments."

"We extract the negative charge of money; in all moments."

"We evaporate the psychic energy related to money; in all moments."

"We extract all of dark money from our light emanation; in all moments."

"We extract all dark money from our sound frequency; in all moments."

"We convert all dark money to divine love to fuel spiritual freedom; in all moments."

The Conversion

There is the idea that having money is a bad thing. Money, as an energy, is neutral. It's as neutral as breath. It is actually the attributes put on money that give it a negative or positive perception and flow. Money is not the root of all evil. The saying is actually the *love* of money is the root of all evil.

Someone who uses their resources to build hospitals, help the poor and have a great life puts a positive spin on money. And someone who uses it to buy drugs, degrade women and indulge in unethical behavior is obviously putting negative attributes on money. The philanthropist has learned the art of creating a fluidity with their financial flow. It is perpetuated with their deeds and intentions.

It may be effective to look at money as an energy flow and to understand how to work with it objectively to perpetuate it in your life. When someone wakes up feeling energetic, they may be inspired to do more with their day but they don't go to extremes. Someone doesn't wake up feeling all energized and say, "I feel really good. I am not going to do anything today so I don't use up this good feeling." They also don't say, "I am feeling so good I am going to go out and run a marathon today to use all this energy up."

What they most likely do is use the energy to do the things they need to do as well as some of the things they like to do. They then expect that the energy level they are feeling will continue to be what it is. By living in this expectancy, they can perpetuate the energetic flow.

It may be helpful to look at the flow of money the same way and treat it accordingly. The Universal law is abundance. If there is not some kind of abundance in your life, you may need to look to yourself for why this is so. Having good health, being very talented, attractive, intelligent, and having love in your life are other forms of abundance. If you take an overview and look at all the blessings in your life as different forms of energy flow, it will be easier to understand how to convert other forms of abundance into income--if that's what is important to you.

The reason so many people go without is that they waste so much of their energy in the pursuit of money. This is not even a lateral move. Your energy is your life force. It is meant to perpetually flow. What happens when you convert your life force into a different form of energy (money), you are taking an infinite well that perpetually flows from your depth and grounding it by converting it into money.

Money can still flow, but we are taught to save it, store it away and be stingy. Doing this takes energy that has always been flowing through your intentions and actions and stops its movement. It becomes stagnant. It is better to keep the energy moving as much as possible. This keeps money flowing closer to the natural state of energy instead of resonating with fear of losing it or being without. The more you can trust money to flow, the more you can treat it like a natural extension of your own energy.

(Say each statement three times out loud while continuously tapping on the top of your head at the crown chakra and say it a fourth time while tapping on your heart chakra.)

"I release converting my abundance to problems; in all moments."

"I release converting my abundance to lack; in all moments."

"I release converting my abundance to loneliness; in all moments."

"I release converting my abundance to dis-ease; in all moments."

"I release converting my abundance to drama; in all moments."

"I release converting my abundance to complaints; in all moments."

"I release converting my abundance to apathy; in all moments."

"I release converting my abundance to unworthiness; in all moments."

"I release converting my abundance to failure; in all moments."

"I release converting my abundance to self-doubt; in all moments."

"I release converting my abundance to sabotage; in all moments."

"I release converting my abundance to depression; in all moments."

"I release converting my abundance to anger; in all moments."

"I release converting my abundance to judgment; in all moments."

"I release converting my abundance to helplessness; in all moments."

"I convert all problems back to abundance; in all moments."

"I convert all lack back to abundance; in all moments."

"I convert all loneliness back to abundance; in all moments."

"I convert all dis-ease back to abundance; in all moments."

"I convert all drama back to abundance; in all moments."

"I convert all complaints back to abundance; in all moments."

"I convert all apathy back to abundance; in all moments."

"I convert all unworthiness back to abundance; in all moments."

"I convert all failure back to abundance; in all moments."

"I convert all self-doubt back to abundance; in all moments."

"I convert all sabotage back to abundance; in all moments."

"I convert all depression back to abundance; in all moments."

"I convert all anger back to abundance; in all moments."

"I convert all judgment back to abundance; in all moments."

"I convert all helplessness back to abundance; in all moments."

"I collect and embrace abundance in all forms; in all moments."

"I am centered and empowered in abundance; in all moments."

"I resonate and emanate abundance; in all moments."

The Illusion of Money

What came through in a session recently was meant for a particular person but may be relevant to others.

Money is the curse. When people don't have money, the Universe is trying to free them from an illusion that has trapped so many for so long. People are being given a gift of not needing it. As they are being gifted, they are disregarding it and crying out for the illusion. So many have traded their connection with the land, family, and contentment for the lie of security and luxury. They have turned their back on the spirits that guide them to follow a wisp of an illusion or a false promise.

Here are some taps to assist:

(Say each statement three times while tapping on your head, and say it a fourth time while tapping on your chest.)

"I release turning my back on my Spirit Guides; in all moments."

"I release being immersed in illusion; in all moments."

"I release converting love to power; in all moments."

"I release being enslaved to illusion; in all moments."

"I release sacrificing the macrocosm for the microcosm; in all moments."

"I reconnect the macrocosm to the microcosm; in all moments."

The Purification of Money

There is a consensus that billionaires run the world by flooding the media with their point of view and buying a group consensus. Money is only one form of wealth. Every single individual is able to conjure up as much energy as a billionaire. The billionaire has just converted their abundance into a monetary supply.

There is a mentality that giving money to the poor creates a welfare system. But they are only taking into consideration one form of abundance. There are so many other forms of abundance that those who lack money are abundant in. Every positive attribute is a form of abundance. What individuals lack in money, they make up for in heart, resilience, kindness, talents, creativity, imagination, etc.

The moment we all realize all the forms of wealth that we carry, and use them all for the common well being of all, no human mind can ever be unwittingly bought and sold again.

Also, the reason that those who are of a healing nature do not have monetary validation is because the vibration of abundance has been so tainted. To agree to money in its current form is perhaps a dangerous way to open up one's self to the corruption that money is systemically used for. The cure would be to cleanse the vibration of money Universally. Perhaps this will create the balance that is currently lacking in society.

(Say three times while tapping on your head and say it a fourth time while tapping on your chest.)

"I declare myself a surrogate for humanity in doing these taps; in all moments."

"All illusion is stripped off of money; in all moments."

"Money and corruption are untangled from each other; in all moments."

"All corruption is converted back to neutrality; in all moments."

"The vibration of money is cleansed of corruption and greed; in all moments."

"All are released from being enslaved to corruption; in all moments."

"All imbalances and dysfunction caused by corruption and greed are released; in all moments."

"All are released from being at the mercy of greed and corruption; in all moments."

"All the suffering inflicted by the synergy between money and greed is removed; in all moments."

"All psychic streams of energy created by the synergy between money and corruption are dissipated; in all moments."

"All vivaxes between money and corruption are removed; in all moments."

"All tentacles between money and corruption are removed; in all moments."

"All portals of corruption opened to money are collapsed and dissolved; in all moments."

"The claws of corruption are removed from the vibration of money; in all moments."

"All exploitation and demigod behavior of corruption due to money are released; in all moments."

"Money is prevented from being used by corruption; in all moments."

"All programming and conditioning that the corruption of money has put on the world are released; in all moments."

"All engrams of corruption and greed are removed from each other and all others; in all moments."

"All energy matrices that embolden corruption to poison money are sent into the light and sound; in all moments."

"All complex energy matrices are escorted into the light and sound that embolden corruption to poison money; in all moments."

"All energy matrices are sent into the Light and Sound that cause money to be used for corruption; in all moments."

"All complex energy matrices are escorted into the light and sound that cause money to be used for corruption; in all moments."

"All energy matrices are sent into the light and sound that cause others to enable greed and corruption in all moments."

"All illusion is stripped off of the corruption of money and all those who perpetuate it; in all moments."

"All masks, walls, and armor are removed from the corruption of money; in all moments."

"All contracts are nullified between money and corruption; in all moments."

"All agendas of corruption and greed put on money are collapsed and dissolved; in all moments."

"All vows and agreements are nullified between money and corruption; in all moments."

"All curses are removed between money and corruption; in all moments."

"All blessings are removed between money and corruption; in all moments."

"All strings and cords are severed between money and corruption; in all moments."

"All karmic ties are dissolved between money and corruption; in all moments."

"All the pain, burden and limitations that the corruption of money has put on the world are removed; in all moments."

"All negative intentions are removed from the sound frequencies of money; in all moments."

"All negative intentions are removed from the light emanations of money; in all moments."

"The paradigm of money and abundance is shifted from negative manifestations and lack, to perpetual joy, love, health, freedom and wholeness; in all moments."

"Money and abundance transcend all negative intentions; in all moments."

Un-conditioning Yourself

Instead of wasting precious energy wishing to make money, use your intentions to manifest your goal. Stop wasting your energy hoping for money to attain what you desire. Bypass the blockage of needing the desire to come through the process of having money. That is the stopgap on your goal.

You don't really want money for money's sake. You want it to attain the things that you desire. So cut out the middleman and instead of wishing for money, set out the intention to achieve your desires in any way that they are gifted to you. If you can understand this, you can realize that the desire for money is merely a feeling of helplessness and wanting to control the Universe.

You can use the taps below to attain any goal. Yes, you can even use it to attain monetary wealth. But try an experiment. Think of something that you have wanted to have if only you had the money to buy it. Do the following exercise with the thing that you wish to buy. Then forget about it. Don't give it any more attention than doing the taps. See if you end up manifesting the thing of your desire through chance, fate, gift or seeming magic.

There is a freedom in achieving what you wish for without having to go through the linear process of attracting the money first. Believing that you just obtain abundance through having money may be putting unnatural limitations on what you will allow yourself to receive, not because you want to be wired this way. It may just be conditioning.

(Say each statement three times while tapping on your head and say it a fourth time while tapping on your chest.)

"I make space in this world to _____; in all moments."

"I remove all blockages to _____; in all moments."

"I stretch my capacity to _____: in all moments."

"I activate the next cause in_____; in all moments"

"I shatter all glass ceilings on _____; in all moments."

"I am worthy and deserve to _____; in all moments."

"I release believing _____ is too good to be true; in all moments."

"I open all portals to _____; in all moments."

"I walk into the reality of _____; in all moments."

"I close all portals to disappointment and unfavorable results; in all moments."

"I infuse _____ into my light emanation and sound frequency; in all moments."

"I am centered and empowered in _____; in all moments."

"I resonate, emanate and am interconnected with all life in _____; in all moments."

You As an Infinite Source of Abundance

We all know the old way of withholding isn't working, so why are so many still so afraid to share their gifts? The way I see it, sharing your gifts is a win-win: a win for the individual and a win for humanity. The old banking system of hoarding all your wealth works against the spiritual law of abundance. So it is with hoarding the abundance of your infinite self.

Abundance is a perpetual fountain that we dip from. It only dries up when we try to cap it and create a stagnant pool out of the plethora. And so it is with our own intangible gifts. They stagnate when they aren't shared. The more you share everything that you are, the more amazing and empowered you will become. This is in accordance with the spiritual law of abundance.

"I am an infinite source of perpetual abundance; in all moments."

"I remove all blockages to being an infinite source of perpetual abundance; in all moments."

"I accept all forms of positive abundance; in all moments."

"I release cock blocking infinite, perpetual abundance; in all moments."

"I release micromanaging the ways that I will accept abundance; in all moments."

"I release thwarting the flow of infinite abundance by fixating on monetary measures; in all moments."

"I release mistrusting the flow of infinite, perpetual abundance working within and for me; in all moments."

"I release the trauma of the illusion of being disconnected with abundance; in all moments."

"I free myself from the illusion of lack; in all moments."

"I free myself from the illusion of want, need and hope; in all moments."

"I release moving away from my center of infinite abundance through want, need or hope; in all moments."

"I release derailing from my center through want, need or hope; in all moments."

"I release deflecting the flow of abundance; in all moments."

"I release inadvertently programming myself for lack; in all moments."

"I shift my paradigm from need to have; in all moments."

"I shift my paradigm from doing to being; in all moments."

"I stretch my capacity for self-love to include infinite, perpetual abundance; in all moments."

"I am centered and empowered in infinite perpetual abundance; in all moments."

"I resonate, emanate and am interconnected with all life in infinite, perpetual abundance; in all moments."

RELEASE ALL YOUR ISSUES IN REGARD TO MONEY

Make a list of every belief you have about money and your relationship with money. Include every limiting thought that you have had about not having enough money and things that you have told yourself about money. If you have worried about paying the bills or always say that you are broke, put those on the list too. Make the list as long as you can, and keep adding to it as much as you can.

Use the following worksheet to add one item on your list to all the blanks and do the whole set of taps with that one issue. Use this worksheet to release all the issues on your list one by one. It is also to write down evidence of receiving abundance out of the blue so that you can document your success. Make a note of when you first start doing the taps and more opportunity for abundance and wealth arrive.

The Energetic Cleanse:

Think of something that annoys you or you have been obsessing over. It can be a job, person, task, relationship, global issue or a habit. After you name the issue, say each statement out loud three times while tapping on the top of your head, and say it a fourth time while tapping on your chest.

"All engrams of _____ are removed; in all moments."

"All vivaxes with _____ are removed; in all moments."

"All tentacles of _____ are removed; in all moments."

"All my energy is withdrawn from _____; in all moments."

"All dependency on _____ is released; in all moments."

65

"Feeling beholden to _____ is eliminated; in all moments."

"All vows and agreements with _____ are recanted; in all moments."

"All contracts with _____ are nullified; in all moments."

"All curses with _____ are removed; in all moments."

"All blessings with _____ are removed; in all moments."

"All strings and cords with _____ are severed; in all moments."

"All karmic ties with _____ are dissolved; in all moments."

"All the pain, burden, limitations and engrams that _____ has inflicted are removed; in all moments."

"All the pain, burden, limitations and engrams that have been caused due to _____ are removed; in all moments."

"All that was taken from _____ is returned; in all moments."

"All the Joy, Love, Abundance, Freedom, Health, Success, Security, Companionship, Creativity, Peace, Life, Wholeness, Beauty, Enthusiasm, Contentment, Spirituality, Enlightenment and Confidence that _____ has taken is returned; in all moments."

"Resonating with _____ is released; in all moments."

"Emanating with _____ is released in; in all moments."

"All of _____ is removed from my sound frequency; in all moments."

"All of _____ is removed from my light emanation; in all moments."

"My paradigm is shifted from _____ to Joy, Love, Abundance, Freedom, Health, Success, Security, Companionship, Creativity, Peace, Life, Wholeness, Beauty, Enthusiasm, Contentment, Spirituality, Enlightenment and Confidence; in all moments."

"All illusion is stripped from _____; in all moments."

"The first cause of enabling _____ is eliminated; in all moments."

"All masks, walls and armor are removed from _____; in all moments."

"All masks, walls and armor that were implemented due to _____ are removed; in all moments."

"All energy matrices of _____ are sent into the Light and Sound; in all moments."

"All complex energy matrices of _____ are escorted into the Light and Sound; in all moments."

"All portals to _____ are collapsed and dissolved; in all moments."

"All of _____ is transcended; in all moments."

"The wei chi of all bodies is repaired; in all moments."

"All bodies are aligned; in all moments."

"All are centered and empowered in Divine Love; in all moments."

Jen Ward

68

PEANUT BUTTER AND JELLY TAPS

These taps are to release two things that are symbiotic from each other and then from you. If peanut butter and jelly no longer wanted to be associated with each other, this is the set of taps they would use. If there are two things that work together to diminish your effectiveness, use this set of taps to release them from you.

For example, if both parents gang up on you, then do this set of taps and put both of their names in the blanks; or if two friends make you feel diminished when you are together; also, if you struggle between two factions, like two different religious beliefs or two different political factions.

How to use this worksheet below:

Make two lists. The first list is all the factions that you believe prevented you from having money--anything that you lament as a reason why you don't have money. There is no wrong answer. It can be things like lack of education, lack of opportunity, social standing, upbringing, lack of support, abuse, starting a family too early. Make the list as long as you can.

The second list is all the things that are a result of not having as much money as you would like. Some examples are a lack of clout, going hungry, being judged, stress, being evicted, lack of freedom, debt, creditors, etc. Make this list as long as you can.

Number both lists. When you have exhausted all the things that you can think of, use the worksheet to do the exercise with every single thing that you wrote in the first list (one at a time) and match it with one of the issues on the second list. Do the exercise with every matchup possible. Start at the top of list one, and do the exercise with it and the first thing you wrote on the second list.

Do the first item on list one with every issue on list two, one by one. Then once you've done the worksheet with every pair-up from list two with the first issue on the first list, move to the second issue on the first list and do THAT issue one by one with every issue on the second list.

This is a way to untangle all your beliefs about lack of money with all your beliefs about why you don't have money. It's a very powerful exercise.

(Say three times while tapping on your head and say a fourth time while tapping on your chest.)

"All imbalances caused by _____ and _____ are released; in all moments."

"All the dysfunction of _____ and _____ is released; in all moments."

"I am released from being at the mercy of _____ and _____; in all moments."

"I am released from being enslaved to _____ and _____; in all moments."

"All the suffering accrued between _____ and _____ is removed; in all moments."

"All the suffering inflicted by _____ and _____ is released; in all moments."

"I am released from being manipulated by _____ and _____; in all moments."

"All vivaxes between _____ and _____ are removed; in all moments."

"All vivaxes between _____ and _____, and myself are removed; in all moments."

"All tentacles between _____ and _____ are removed; in all moments."

"All tentacles between _____ and _____, and myself are removed; in all moments."

"The claws of _____ and _____ are removed from each other's essence; in all moments."

"The claws of _____ and _____ are removed from my essence; in all moments."

"All injustice and inequality between_____ and _____ are removed; in all moments."

"All injustice and inequality between_____ and _____ , and myself are removed; in all moments."

"All exploitive and demigod interactions between _____ and _____ are released; in all moments."

"_____ and _____ release feeding off of each other; in all moments."

"_____ and _____ release feeding off of me; in all moments."

"All programming and conditioning that _____ and _____ have put on each other are released; in all moments."

"All programming and conditioning that _____ and _____ have put on me are released; in all moments."

"All engrams of _____ and _____ are removed from each other; in all moments."

"All engrams of _____ and _____ are removed from me; in all moments."

"All energy matrices are sent into the Light and Sound that cause
_____ and _____ to diminish each other; in all
moments."

"All energy matrices are sent into the Light and Sound that cause
_____ and _____ to take from me; in all
moments."

"All complex energy matrices are commanded to be escorted into
the Light and Sound that cause _____ and
_____ to diminish each other; in all moments."

"All complex energy matrices are commanded to be escorted into
the Light and Sound that cause _____ and
_____ to take from me; in all moments."

"All energy matrices are sent into the Light and Sound that cause
_____ and _____ to cling to each other; in all
moments."

"All energy matrices are sent into the Light and Sound that cause
_____ and _____ to cling to me; in all
moments."

"All complex energy matrices are commanded to be escorted into
the Light and Sound that cause _____ and
_____ to cling to each other; in all moments."

"All complex energy matrices are commanded to be escorted into
the Light and Sound that cause _____ and
_____ to cling to me; in all moments."

"All energy matrices are sent into the Light and Sound that cause
_____ and _____ to stay together; in all
moments."

"All complex energy matrices are commanded to be escorted into
the Light and Sound that cause _____ and
_____ to stay with me; in all moments."

"All illusion is stripped off of _____ and _____;
in all moments."

"All masks, walls, and armor are removed between _____
and _____; in all moments."

"All masks, walls, and armor are removed from _____
and _____; in all moments."

"All blinders are removed from _____ and
_____; in all moments."

"All contracts are nullified between _____ and
_____; in all moments."

"All contracts are nullified between _____ and
_____, and me; in all moments."

"All engrams and all agendas that _____ and
_____ have put on me are removed; in all moments."

"All vows and agreements are nullified between _____
and _____; in all moments."

"All vows and agreements are nullified between _____
and _____, and me; in all moments."

"All curses are removed between _____ and
_____; in all moments."

"All curses are removed that _____ and _____
have put on me; in all moments."

"All blessings are removed between _____ and
_____; in all moments."

"All blessings are removed that _____ and
_____ have put on me; in all moments."

"All strings and cords are severed between _____ and
_____; in all moments."

"All karmic ties are dissolved between _____ and _____; in all moments."

"All the pain, burden and limitations that _____ and _____ have put on each other are removed; in all moments."

"All the pain, burden and limitations that _____ and _____ have put on me are removed; in all moments."

"All the illusion of inadequacies, rejection, abandonment and separation that _____ and _____ have put on each other are removed; in all moments."

"All the illusion of inadequacies, rejection, abandonment and separation that _____ and _____ have put on me are removed; in all moments."

"All that _____ and _____ have taken from each other, is returned; in all moments."

"All that _____ and _____ have taken from me, is returned; in all moments."

"All the genetic propensity for dis-ease that _____ and _____ have put on me, is removed; in all moments."

"I release resonating with the dysfunction of _____ and _____; in all moments."

"I release emanating with the dysfunction of _____ and _____; in all moments."

"All need and dysfunction of _____ and _____ are removed from my Sound Frequency; in all moments."

"All need and dysfunction of _____ and _____ are removed from my Light emanations; in all moments."

"My paradigm is shifted from the dysfunction of _____ and _____ to perpetual Joy, Love, Abundance Freedom and Wholeness; in all moments."

"I transcend all the need and dysfunction of _____ and _____; in all moments."

"I am centered and empowered in perpetual Joy, Love, Abundance Freedom and Wholeness; in all moments."

"I resonate, emanate, and m interconnected with each other and all life in perpetual Joy, Love, Abundance, Freedom, and Wholeness; in all moments."

Jen Ward

GLOSSARY OF TERMS

There are some very complicated metaphysical concepts that do not need to be so difficult to understand. Anything that is fathomable in the Universe should be able to be simplified so a child can understand them. For instance, there are no words that explain the energy pull between two things. That would be the word vivaxes. As we become more enlightened, we will need more and more words to explain our ever-expanding relationship with energy.

Claws: Sometimes and in some instances, one will feel psychically gripped by an issue. The best way to depict the feeling of this is with the word claws.

Engrams: Engrams are the way that past issues are stored in our energy field. Think of how a groove in a vinyl record plays a song repeatedly when a needle is inserted in the groove. An engram is a groove in your energy field that plays a behavior repeatedly.

Enlightenment: The formula process of meeting all of the negativity within you and stripping it away so one is no longer at the mercy of the ego and sees one more as a reflection of the higher realms than in reactionary mode.

Light Bodies: We seem like solid energy. But we are really made of layers of energy consisting of different vibrations. Our physical body is the coarsest. Then the emotions create a layer of vibration around that. People know that layer as the astral level of vibration. Then there is the level that contains the memory of every past experience. This layer is called the causal plane and the records are called the akashic records. After that layer of vibration is the mental realm. This is the same layer as the ego and it is why it is difficult to see beyond the mental realm because the ego tries to prevent it. Above that level, the duality of the lower vibrations is dropped and then energy beyond that is one of such purity, it registers as a neutrality. That is why feeling good is not the highest expression of love, but loving neutrality or detachment is a more spiritual state. The ego will convey this as bliss but in its true state, it is neither positive nor negative.

Light Emanation: We are not solid matter. In energy, we are a light emanation and a sound frequency woven together to give the illusion of matter.

Matrix (pl. matrices): Stagnant energy can exist in cloud form. We walk through it all the time during the day. It can affect our moods. If we walk through energy and it identifies with our vibration, it may collect in us as individuals and seem like an intrusion.

Complex Energy Matrix: When an energy matrix intrudes upon your energy system and identifies itself with a personality. It may convince you and it that it is an aspect of you or that it is a totally different individual that has taken you over in some way. It is merely stagnant energy that needs to be dissipated. No melodrama necessary. Just release it with the taps

Portal: An energetic gateway.

Psychic Stream of Energy: A compilation of a similar vibration of thoughts and emotions that creates a cloud like energy that can affect those who are subjected to it.

Sound Frequency: One of the two aspects of ourselves, the other one being Light emanation. All energy is either Light or Sound. Knowing ourselves as Sound Frequencies and Light Emanations is breaking ourselves down to our true state devoid of ego and ego limitations. It is as a Sound Frequency or Light Emanation that we are capable of traveling in all realms and knowing ourselves as Omniscient, Omnipotent and Omnipresent. It is also a means of communicating with Source or God in its native tongue.

Strings: When two energy sources touch, a string of connecting energy is formed between them. If attention is kept on this string, it can become reinforced with obsessive or repetitive thoughts. These strings need to be broken if one is going to be free of the object of the taps.

Tentacle: Energy that reaches out and attaches to someone perhaps to take from them or feed off their energy.

Vivaxis: An energy pull between two or more people, places or things.

Vortex: A vortex is an energy pull similar to a gravitational pull between two components. For example, there is a vortex between the sun and all the planets and there is a vortex between the earth and moon.

Wei chi: The "skin" on the surface of your energy field that provides a natural barrier to energies interrupting your natural function. It gets pierced and broken during trauma and then it is more difficult for an energy to hold its electromagnetic charge. Someone whose wei chi is in tact may have a natural magnetism.

www.jenuinehealing.com/sft-dictionary/

Jen Ward

ABOUT THE AUTHOR

Jen Ward is an Ascended Master. This entails being a Reiki Master, gifted healer, inspirational speaker, author of many books and an innovator of a healing modality for self-empowerment. She offers a simple but dynamic protocol to assist individuals in clearing up all their energy imbalances (karma) with every person, experience, belief system and the Universe. She enables all those struggling, to cross the bridge of self-discovery, with her encouragement and instruction. Her passion is to empower the world by encouraging all individuals in their own miraculous healing adventure.

Jen is considered a sangoma, a traditional African shaman who channels ancestors, and clears energy by emoting sounds and vocalizations. An interesting prerequisite to being a sangoma is to have survived being on the brink of death. When it was first revealed that Jen was a sangoma, she had not yet fulfilled the rigorous prerequisites necessary. However, in April 2008, through a series of traumas, she returned to civilization meeting all the requirements. She passed through the transforming process of enlightenment. She returned to the world of humanity a devout soul inspired to serve.

Jen currently works diligently in the physical world and in the worlds of energy to assist all souls to reach greater heights of awareness and empowerment. Those who believe they have "arrived," may be the most entrenched in the mental realms. They can painlessly free themselves without relinquishing the comfort of their current belief system. All that needs to be released will fall away naturally. "Fear, in all its subtle forms of denial and judgment, will naturally fall away."

Many people report receiving healing assistance from Jen or protection in the dream state and even more subtle realms. Jen is passionate to shatter the mentality of sitting at the feet of another. She shares truth and wisdom graciously and abundantly. Jen makes the practice of doling out truth in increments to set up the dynamic of personality worship obsolete. Her passion is to assist the world over the brink of all perceived limitations, beyond the mind's scope, into the realms of enlightenment.

OTHER BOOKS BY JEN WARD

Enlightenment Unveiled: Expound into Empowerment. This book contains case studies to help you peel away the layers to your own empowerment using the tapping technique.

Grow Where You Are Planted: Quotes for an Enlightened "Jeneration." Inspirational quotes that are seeds to shift your consciousness into greater awareness.

Perpetual Calendar: Daily Exercises to Maintain Balance and Harmony in Your Health, Relationships and the Entire World. 369 days of powerful taps to use as a daily grounding practice for those who find meditation difficult.

Children of the Universe. Poetry to Elevate the Reader to the 5th Dimension. Passionate prose to lead the reader lovingly into expanded consciousness.

Letters of Accord: Assigning Words to Unspoken Truth. Truths that the ancient ones want you to know to redirect your life and humanity back into empowerment.

The Do What You Love Diet: Finally, Finally, Finally, Feel Good in Your Own Skin. Revolutionary approach to regaining fitness by tackling primal imbalances in relationship to food.

Emerging from the Mist: Awakening the Balance of Female Empowerment in the World. Release all the issues that prevent someone from embracing their female empowerment.

Affinity for All Life: Valuing Your Relationship with All Species. This book is a means to strengthen and affirm your relationship with the animal kingdom.

The Wisdom of the Trees. If one is struggling for purpose, they can find love, and truth by tuning into the Wisdom of the Trees.

Chronicles of Truth. Truth has been buried away for way too long. Here is a means to discover the truth that lies dormant within yourself.

Healing Your Relationships. This book is a means to open up communications and responsiveness to others so that clarity and respect can flourish again in society.

How to Awaken Your Inner Dragon: Visualizations to Empower Yourself and the World. Tap into the best possible version of you and the world.

Collecting Everyday Miracles: Commit to Being Empowered. This book is a thought provoking means to recreate the moment of conception with everyday miracles. It is through gratitude and awareness. This is what this book fosters.

The SFT Lexicon: Spiritual Freedom Technique. Tap into the powerful ability of the mind to self-heal.

Past Lives, Dreams and Inspiration. People are starving for truth. Unfortunately, they have been conditioned to dismiss their dreams and all remnants of past lives in discovering their own trajectory connection to truth. This book gives life to the expansiveness of self-discovery through one's past lives and dream experiences. There is no greater form of inspiration than discovering one's own depth.

2018 A Turning Point: Shift from Primal Mode to Enlightenment. If in 2018 you sensed a shift in the world, if you sensed an internal struggle happening on the world's behalf, if you are fascinated with truths that are hidden from the masses, or if you have some programming left that you would like to eliminate, this book is for you.

God: The Ultimate Search Engine. Finally a book to address all the layers of shame piled on the individual in the name of a vengeful, petty God. Man has spoken for God long enough. It's time to speak to God directly.

All of Jen's books can be found on her website at JenuineHealing.com.

www.ingramcontent.com/pod-product-compliance
Lightning Source LLC
Chambersburg PA
CBHW020556030426
42337CB00013B/1115